Look Deep and Leap

Finding Your Passion and Purpose

Look Deep and Leap

Finding Your Passion and Purpose

Lorena Fiore

Real with Lorena
www.RealWithLorena.com

Look Deep and Leap

Finding Your Passion and Purpose

Copyright © 2015 by Lorena Fiore

The content of this book is for general instruction only. Each person's physical, emotional, and spiritual condition is unique. The instruction in this book is not intended to replace or interrupt the reader's relationship with a physician or other professional. Please consult your doctor for matters pertaining to your specific health and diet.

ISBN 978-0-9961300-0-4

Printed in the United States of America

To Mom and Dad

You are my first and

most enduring teachers.

Through your example,

I have learned to love

with an open heart and

to trust without judgement.

TABLE OF CONTENTS

"It's never too late to be what
you might have been."
—GEORGE ELLIOT

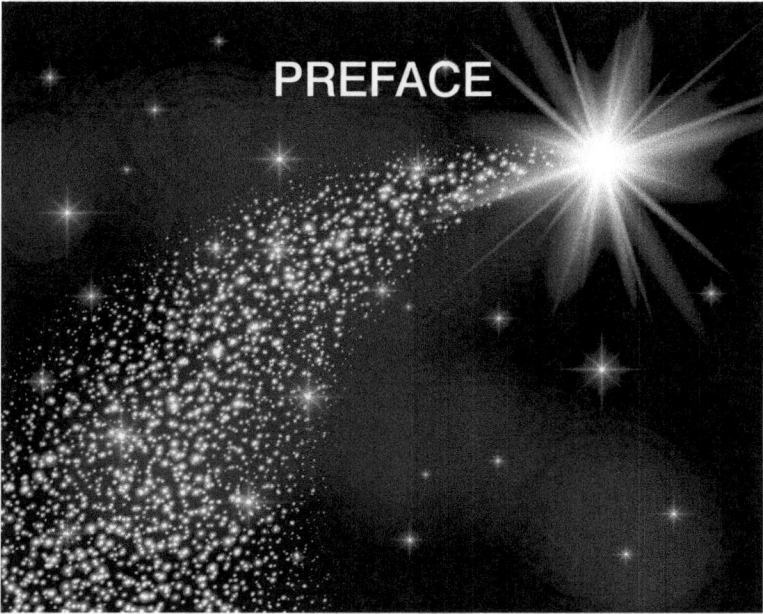

PREFACE

I've felt a kind of restlessness for much of my life. Even during my happiest times, I felt like there was something else that I should be doing. I read books like: What color is your parachute? I attended classes; I received certificates. I even attempted to start my own business. But I never seemed to follow through. I had a wonderful career as a nurse and later as an educator, followed by a sales career. I had two beautiful sons and a large family and circle of friends.

So why didn't I feel a sense of contentment?

Just like everyone else, I've experienced the pain of separation and I've had my share of challenges throughout but I've also experienced much love and laughter. After many years of searching and sometimes wondering if I would ever figure things out for myself, I finally came to a place that truly felt like home.

It is my hope that contained in the following pages; you too, will find your own path to fulfillment. I'll share some truths and insights that I've gained throughout my personal journey and hopefully, my words will create a spark within you to begin your own personal journey.

I wrote the following poem one summer day while I was sitting in my sun porch, looking out at my beautiful pond, contemplating life. I share it with you now.

Stretching, reaching, ever so far
Breaking through to a distant star
I need to get there, to make it right
I'll not stop till I find my light!

It guides my path and makes it clear
I'm almost there; it's oh, so near!
I've found it now: I'm here at last
Here is my future, my key to the past

I look to the star for my answers to life
To end all my pain, and struggle and strife
But to my surprise, when I come face to face
With this beautiful star in this magical place

I find that my journey to hear its sweet song
Was never the answer; it was mine all along
For when I crept closer on bended knee
That beautiful star, so brilliant, was me!

"I have noticed even people who claim everything is predestined, and that we can do nothing to change it, look before they cross the road."
—STEPHEN HAWKING

INTRODUCTION

Getting Clear

What do you believe? What's really important for you? Are you living your life aligned with those beliefs? We're bombarded day by day, minute by minute by messages telling us what we should eat, what we should buy, how we should look, how much money we should be earning, saving and spending. We're put into neat little categories and grouped and labeled.

We have an endless supply of choices and there is a plethora of information, much of it contradictory and confusing. Think about it, we now can spend days agonizing over what phone to buy and when that's finally determined, what plan should we buy? Glad to have that checked off your list?

Wait a minute; what apps are you going to download into it? You get the picture. And this is just one example: Internet banking or brick & mortar banking? Mac or PC? Satellite TV or cable TV?

Our world is rapidly growing and expanding and all of these advancements and quick access to information is amazing yet it can be overwhelming, time consuming and draining. It can fill our psyche so full that we have no time to simply "be," time to reflect and time to breathe, time to stay still and listen, time to be grateful, to love, to laugh, to balance, to be truly whole. And until we are whole, we will be stuck. This can manifest itself in many different ways. We can be stuck in our own heads: "I'm not good enough," "I'm not young enough, thin enough, smart enough." We can be stuck and not even realize it because we haven't taken the time to simply be aware and be still:

unhealthy relationships, dead end jobs, lucrative jobs that don't resonate with us.

It is my belief that every one of us has a unique, amazing gift to offer to this world. And when we realize this gift and move forward to share it, we not only enrich others but we give ourselves the realization of who we truly are and that, my friend, is our true purpose. It is why we are all here on this planet.

So yes, look at the possibilities, look at the pros and cons of moving forward, of making that change no matter how small. But more than that, look inside. Look into your soul. Listen to your voice. It is my hope that I can help you in this endeavor by exploring all of the ways that we can find true balance within ourselves. We all share a common desire to be in balance and as we move closer to it, our voice becomes a little clearer, our hearts open a little wider and we intuitively move toward our purpose.

Your Road Map

I'll ask you to look at yourself a little more intently to help you gain some insight and understanding about what you're doing or not doing and why. We will explore all of the areas of your life that make you who you are and that shape your experiences. Each of these areas contributes to the whole of who you are at this moment. And so each deserves our attention.

We'll start with your physical body. What are you putting into your body for nourishment and how are you giving it the movement it needs? Next, we'll look at your daily life in terms of what you do: your chosen occupation, your daily routine. We'll then move into relationships, both external and internal. This is an important area and one that can uncover hidden fears that may be holding you back. Lastly, we'll look at your belief system in terms of your spirituality. Each section is independent of the other so feel free to read these chapters in whatever order you choose. There are thought provoking questions throughout and I encourage you to pause and carefully consider each question to get the most benefit from them. I've included blank pages at the end of the book for you to write down your thoughts as they occur. Consider using these pages for moments of clarity and inspiration as well.

As you read these pages, open your mind and heart to new discovery and possibility. And know that we're all on this beautiful journey together. So smile and enjoy. I know I am as I write these words to you.

"Tell me what you eat, and
I will tell you who you are."
—BRILLAT-SAVIRIN

CHAPTER ONE

What Are You Hungry For?

Cereal, Toast and Coffee

What did your diet look like today? How about yesterday, last week or last month? Chances are your answers will be the same or at least very similar on most days. We seem to get comfortable with a core group of meals and we just keep repeating these meals over and over. We eat mindlessly and tend to gravitate to what is convenient and familiar. I know I did! Every day for many years, my standard breakfast was a bowl of cereal, one slice of toast with peanut butter and jelly and a cup of black coffee. This was the meal I started my day with no matter what else was going on for me. I counted on it to be there every day. I could just get up and have it without worrying about what I should have. It provided me with a sense of security, a familiar, time tested breakfast that provided me with a sense of comfort. I enjoyed it and it's not necessarily a bad breakfast choice so what's the problem? Well, I love carbs and there lie my conundrum. I suffered with IBS for many years, some years worse than others. And finally after seeking relief from several different practitioners, it was discovered that my body doesn't process carbohydrates very effectively. I was left questioning, "What? How about my bread, my cereals, my pasta? What am I supposed to eat for breakfast now?" This was going to be a challenge!

As daunting as this seemed at the time, I knew I had to make changes. I did work through it with the aid of digestive enzymes and some major diet tweaking (including going gluten free) and I'm happy to report that I now experience relief from my symptoms and I've gained more energy in the process. Needless to say, my daily breakfast routine is no more. I do still occasionally enjoy my peanut butter and jelly, though now it's almond butter. And guess what? I've discovered so many new and wonderful foods that I never would have considered before. I now enjoy foods like smoothies and home made porridge to start my day and beyond breakfast, the rest of my day is filled with new foods as well. Discovering and trying new foods has led me to experiment and try new recipes. I love creating healthy delicious meals for myself and for my family. And through this process, I've opened myself up more to the idea of change, of challenge and new directions.

Now I know that this particular breakfast was about more than my food preference. It was my daily, reliable routine. Having that routine disrupted forced me to make a change that ultimately created anxiety for me. When I look back now at this breakfast that I ate for so many years I think, "This meal, this tiny portion of my daily life, represented just that: my life, safe and sure."

But life is much more. So many of us are just going

through the motions. Yes, we have our moments of real happiness but I'm talking about feeling joyous and energized every day. We wonder if we're missing something, if we've made wrong choices. Why do we feel so stuck? I have a mantra that I always say to myself when I'm feeling stuck and that's *Action creates reaction*. So in other words, if you do nothing or change nothing, things will remain exactly as they are. Recognizing this is simple. Determining how we can change this scenario is the difficult part. How do we challenge ourselves to be better, to be happy and in doing so, spread that happiness to others? One small step, that's the answer, plain and simple. And I know you've heard it many times before. What exactly does that mean for you?

I ask you now to think about your food choices. Are they predictable? Are they convenient? Beyond that, try to look at the why of your food choices. Does this food make you happy when you're down? Does that choice stuff down all of your bad feelings when you feel overwhelmed? Do you eat this because, damn it, you deserve it even if you don't think you should be eating it? Just look, look inside and see what you see. What you do with the information is up to you. What do you really want? How do you want to feel? What is your end goal? Please take the time to do this for yourself. I know this can be tough stuff for many of you. Food is so much more than food. It can represent all the things I talked about and more.

For me, it represented safety and security and when I had to disrupt that, it was overwhelming at first. But through the process of that change, I grew and it was my first small step. Food can be love; it can be your companion. Look and listen within and you will hear what you need to hear. I want you to enjoy your food and to have fun discovering new foods to prepare. And at the same time I want you to be healthy and ready to take on your life at full throttle! So let's talk about food, shall we?

Help! What Should I eat?

Food, there is so…much information surrounding this topic! What foods are good or bad for us, what foods make us fat, give us diabetes, heartburn, or contribute to hypertension? And then there's the myriad of available diets, all claiming to have the solution for whatever ails you. It is not my intent to give you your specific solution or to fill you with lots of facts and statistics. I will, however, give you solid guidelines to live by that will nourish your body in a loving way.

Before I get to that, I do want to acknowledge again that we are all unique individuals and as such what's good for one may be problematic for another. So be mindful of what you're eating and how it may be affecting you, both positively and negatively. You are the true expert for your body. You intuitively know the best fuel for it if you simply pay attention to its signals. Notice any changes in energy level, skin issues, gut issues or mental clarity. Food affects our entire body. It can and does affect each unique gene expression. Know that whatever food enters your body is more than just something to satiate your hunger. It is your vital source of fuel. It can heal you and enable you to thrive. It's wonderful in its variety and possibilities. Enjoy it, experiment with it, have fun with it! It shouldn't be a source of stress and confusion. And when you sit down to eat your chosen foods, think mindfully about where this food came from and be grateful for it. Eat slowly and deliberately.

When I was growing up we always had family dinners together. Everyone talked about his or her day and it was a time to reconnect. We told stories, we laughed and we shared. No matter what was going on for each of us individually, we always ate this meal together as a family. When I think about these meals today, I think of them with appreciation and love. Though I didn't know it then, these times together were helping me to become whole. They were feeding me much more than food; they were nourishing me with love and a sense of belonging. We're all so rushed today and moving in so many directions at once. We have meetings and practices, errands and assignments, obligations and appointments. We are starved for time to spend together! Please try to spend as many family meals together as you can. It will help you to develop a sense of who you are as a family and that's really what it's all about, this connection, and not so much about the food.

For all of you who live alone and for all of you that may live with someone and still find yourself eating alone, remember this. You deserve a delicious meal eaten with awareness and enjoyed fully. I have had many meals by myself and I can say that I have managed to avoid eating in front of a television set and have even occasionally, bought some flowers for the table because I am worth it. We are all worth it. Be good to yourself. Your body holds the very essence of who you are and you need it to carry you throughout this journey we're all on. So treat it kindly and nourish it.

At this point you're probably asking yourself exactly what foods you should be eating and what foods would be best to avoid. Ask that question to ten different people, including leading "experts" on this subject and you'll likely get ten different answers. There are countless theories and diets available to you, so many that it's downright confusing! Meat or no meat, high carb or high protein, low fat or high healthy fats, you get the picture! And then there's the question of when to eat. Some people swear by three meals a day with nothing to eat after 8:00 p.m. Others refer to themselves as grazers who prefer to eat smaller amounts frequently throughout the day. Add to that the fact that the advice keeps changing. Remember when we all thought margarine was a healthy alternative to butter? Please listen to your own body. You know intuitively what you need to eat to feel your best. Keep a food diary and record everything you eat and drink, along with how you're feeling. Are you energetic? Anxious? Tired? Achy? Pay close attention and you may see a pattern emerge that will guide you in your food selection.

For those of you who are experiencing physical issues and aren't exactly sure what's causing them, an elimination diet is a wonderful tool. Some refer to this as a Cleanse. I got to the root of my digestive issues by doing this. There are many different elimination diets with varying degrees of abstinence from certain foods and for different lengths of time. Many suggest supplementation while you're going through the process. It's not my purpose to recommend a particular one but I do want you to be aware that they do exist as an option, if you feel you could benefit from one. Basically, you eliminate certain foods for a period of time. These foods often include gluten, sugar, dairy, nightshades, soy, coffee or anything that you think may be contributing to the problem. Then when the elimination period is over you reintroduce each food one at a time and record any reactions. This will uncover any foods that may be problematic for you.

What I'm saying to you is: Take control of your body and what foods you choose to put into it. Aren't you tired of listening to all of the outside sources telling you what to eat? I know I am! Yes, there is some sound information out there but you have to filter through a lot of misinformation to get to it and the bottom line is we are all individual. I know I'm repeating myself but it's worth repeating. If you want to try a particular diet, go for it! But please don't take it at face value. Put it to the test and pay close attention to how it is affecting you.

I do want to encourage you to eat real food. Really take the time to look the next time you're in the produce aisle. There are so many fruits and vegetables available to us now that were once virtually unknown. We tend to buy the same foods over and over again. Step outside of your comfort zone. Just try one new food and come up with a way to prepare it. You'll be surprised at just how much you've been missing.

Most likely you've heard the advice to eat organically and/or locally grown food whenever possible. Both of these are great suggestions. Have you ever considered starting your own backyard food garden? You'd be amazed at how much food you can produce in a small space. Your local farmers markets are a great opportunity to buy fresh food at reasonable prices. I know for some of you it's a financial burden to buy organically grown produce; don't beat yourself up about it! When possible, try to buy organic when choosing from the "Top Dirty Dozen" which contain the highest amounts of pesticides. Currently these are (in descending order): apples, strawberries, grapes, celery, peaches, spinach, sweet bell peppers, nectarines-imported, cucumbers, cherry tomatoes, snap peas-imported and potatoes. Conversely, there is a "Clean Fifteen" list, foods that contain the least amount of pesticides. These are: avocadoes, sweet corn, pineapples, cabbage, sweet peas-frozen, onions, asparagus, mangoes, papayas, kiwis, eggplant, grapefruit, cantaloupe, cauliflower and sweet potatoes. The next time you're in your local grocery store shop in the outside aisles. This is where the real food is.

When you do find yourself in the inside aisles, please, read labels. I know you've most likely heard this advice before but do you know what you're looking for? First of all, how many ingredients are in the package you're holding? The shorter the list, the healthier it's going to be. Are there ingredients listed that you don't understand? Chances are these are additives placed there to increase the shelf life of the product and not for your nutritional benefit. Now look at the sugar content. I try to keep this to four grams or less as much as possible. Just by being aware of sugar content and keeping it as low as possible, you will be making a huge improvement in your health. I'm not just talking about things like cookies and cereals here either. Sugars are added to just about every packaged product in your grocery store. There is a wide range of sugar grams in products like jelly and pasta sauce. Pay attention to this. I promise you it will make a difference. Lastly, look at sodium grams, especially if you or someone you prepare food for, has high blood pressure or any form of heart disease. There are plenty of options out there that aren't loaded with sodium. Again, you just have to educate yourself by reading labels! Eventually, you'll find brands that are good choices for you. So, buy fresh, real foods as much as possible and buy organic when you can. When you are buying packaged foods, buy products that have limited amounts of ingredients listed and are low in sugar and sodium.

Many of us are going gluten free for various reasons. For those with celiac disease, it's absolutely vital. For others that believe that they're gluten intolerant, troubling symptoms may ease. Many others have experimented with going gluten free, just to see if they have more energy or feel any difference in their well being at all. This is certainly evident in the abundance of gluten free products that are now readily available. Whatever your reason, I want to caution you that just because it's gluten free, that does not mean that it is healthy.

First of all, what exactly is gluten? It's actually a

protein and it's found in grains such as wheat, rye, barley and spelt. It gives elasticity to dough, helping it rise and keep its shape. Remember our discussion about each individual's unique needs? This holds true for those of you who are avoiding gluten as well. Be aware of your body and your reactions, if any, to gluten. If you do decide that gluten free is the answer for you, the same guidelines for choosing beneficial foods apply here. After all, you're choosing to forego gluten to improve your health. Such a change requires added effort and most likely, added expense. Choose wisely! There are so many gluten free foods on the shelves right now and many of them are not healthy. First and foremost, just like fat-free foods, gluten-free foods can be loaded with refined sugars. Read labels! Also, watch for any added ingredients that you really don't need. The shorter the ingredient list is, the healthier the food. Keep this in mind when you're choosing. Make sense? These gluten-free alternatives may also contain ingredients that can be inflammatory themselves. Be mindful of corn and soy. Pay attention to how they may be affecting you. I, for one, have discovered that I don't do well with corn at all and as a result, I now avoid it. My final word of advice here is to be mindful of the total calorie count in relationship to the nutritional value. You certainly don't want to purchase a product high in calories that contains very little in the way of nutrition. The basis of a gluten-free diet is identical to any diet you choose to adopt: Your food choices should be real food such as fruits and vegetables, lean meats and fish whenever possible. Limit packaged foods!

Don't get overwhelmed with all of the information that's available to you. Follow the guidelines that I've provided and decide for yourself. Please, when any particular food comes into the spotlight for being a new super-food, don't just run out and buy it! Do your research! And if you do decide it's right for you, pay attention. It's your body and no one else knows it as you do. Discover what foods nourish you and above all, enjoy! We have so many wonderful foods to choose from and a variety of ways to prepare them. Have fun experimenting with them! The energy and love that you feel when you prepare foods for yourself and for your family and friends will be transferred into the food. And that's an amazing feeling. Don't you think?

One final thought I'd like to leave you with is that we live in a world that is too often concerned with having the perfect body which can cause some of us to become obsessed with food. We've all heard the phrase: Beauty comes from within. We know this intellectually but it still hurts when we look in the mirror and dislike what we see. What do we do about this? For starters, remember that beauty is subjective. While one person may believe that you're beautiful, another may view you as simply ordinary. What I believe is that it is your own self- perception that matters. If you don't believe you're beautiful, why should anyone else? A person who is open and allows him/herself to be exposed to the world possesses a beauty that supersedes the constraints of their physicality. These people are the ones we all love to be around. They make us feel good; they exude love and warmth. They are beautiful.

Absolutely pay attention to what you're eating, read labels and choose wisely. But don't allow it to be so much a part of your life that instead of nourishing your body, you're creating another stressor. We should feel good when we're eating. We're fueling our perfect bodies so that we will have all the energy we need to share our wonderful gift with the world.

"Movement is the song
of the body."
—VANDA SCARAVELLI

CHAPTER TWO

Did You Say Exercise?

Why Am I Winded?

How much activity have you experienced recently? Do you even think about it? Are you someone who follows a regular schedule at your gym? Do you play an organized sport? Perhaps you spend a lot of time working in your garden. It's not how you choose to incorporate this movement that matters. It's that you do incorporate it in a form that's right for you everyday. Our bodies crave this movement; they need it. It's the natural flow of our being and if you're spending a lot of your time sitting (at your desk or in front of a TV), you're depriving yourself of that flow. Begin by looking at yourself and your daily routine. You'll know if this area of your life needs attention. Simply bringing your awareness to this will start the process. Let me tell you a story about myself.

One morning after I dropped my youngest son off at preschool, I arrived home and decided to take a long walk in my neighborhood. About fifteen minutes into this walk, I just decided to try running. How hard could it be? Well, I ran for about three minutes and was totally winded! This was an unpleasant surprise and it concerned me because I felt like I was a healthy and active 27 year old. On this day my lifelong routine of moving my body on a regular basis began. I went from a walking/running routine to running regularly in local road races. I'm not running races anymore and my activity of choice varies from year to year but my point here is that I always have an activity. And do you know why? Yes, it helps me to stay healthy and it really helps when I'm stressed out but over the years I've come to realize that I move my body because when I do, I feel like I am in control. I am controlling how fast my body moves or how much weight I'm going to lift. In those moments when I'm in the flow of movement, I'm concentrating on the movement only and it's a very centering process for me. I am in the moment.

When my dad was diagnosed with lung cancer I went straight to the gym. I ran and ran, and ran some more. And when I was running, in my mind I was beating his cancer for him. When I got the call I felt totally helpless but for a brief time on that treadmill, I was able to DO something! (I'm happy to report that post surgery he is still here with us). Movement has helped me to get through divorce, sickness, an untimely lay off and many other stressful events that the majority of us will experience. And I believe it can do the same for you!

Let's Move!

Don't you think we all sit too much? Between our televisions, our computers and all of our electronic gadgets, we have lost the joy of movement. Get outside and take a walk; just open the door. It doesn't cost anything. You don't need any special equipment or talent. Just take that first step. Being outside is a wonderfully centering experience. Breathe the air in, feel the air on your face. Listen, really listen to the sounds: birds singing, the rustle of a squirrel or a chipmunk scurrying by, the sound of the wind or a dog barking in the distance. What do you hear? Just be in the moment; be part of the whole experience. We're so busy rushing here and there we forget how to let go. Even when our bodies aren't rushing our heads are. We're making lists and thinking about things that have happened or may happen in the future. It's so important to sometimes just let it go, even for just a few short moments. Hey, I know it's hard! I'm constantly figuring things out in my head. But you know what? Throughout the day, when I catch myself thinking too hard, I pull my shoulders down, open up my chest and take a long deep breath, hold and then slowly exhale. It feels amazing! It's calming and guaranteed to bring you back into focus and relaxation. Do it when you're stuck in traffic or when you're waiting in a line that seems far too long. Because the truth is, we all need to take the time to practice self- love, for the good of our bodies and our psyches. So the next time you feel stressed out, annoyed, overwhelmed or just a bit on edge, take that deep breath! And if possible in that moment, move your body: stretch, pull, push, flow, move!

Look inside again and this time ask yourself, "How much do I move each day and how much time do I spend sitting? Is there a reason I'm not moving more? What will happen if I do create more movement? What do I want to have happen?" Notice I am not using the word exercise in this discussion. I love to exercise and it's a word that means joy, happiness and good health. It also can mean sweating, sacrifice, hard effort and sore muscles. For those of you who already exercise regularly and love it, this word will undoubtedly not conjure up any anxiety for you but for those of you who resist it, I use the word movement because this is the natural flow or direction of our bodies and hopefully, our lives. And even for you exercisers out there, a thoughtful introspection on movement can be beneficial for you as well. Because as wonderful as those sessions in the gym or those organized sports activities are for you, it's how you incorporate movement into your everyday life when you're not in your exercise routine that will stay with you for your lifetime and keep you limber and active well into your later years.

I'd like to share an observation with you now that has perplexed me for a long time. (Actually, I've had more than one chuckle about it.) It demonstrates this idea of incorporating movement beautifully. Gym parking lots are often crowded, especially during certain times of the day. And at any given time, I'll see cars going around and around waiting for that spot that's closer to the door. There may be spaces farther out but these eager gym goers don't take them. These same people are there for the sole purpose of getting exercise but they want to walk the shortest distance possible to and from their cars. How's that for irony? Movement should be an expected and even anticipated event in our daily lives.

When you wake up in the morning, before you get out of bed, take that deep breath to relax and prepare for your day. Then stretch, that's right, as far as you can. Stretch your fingers and your toes, your legs, your arms, your torso. Have you ever observed a cat when they awaken? They always stretch before they move. They do this intuitively and so should we. It creates a few precious moments for each of us and helps prepare us for our day.

Beyond stretching, walking is great for all of us. It strengthens our hearts and our bones and if it's done outside it's even better. There's something about walking outside, even if it's not in a lush forest or on a sandy beach. It makes us feel more alive, don't you think?

Just as with food, when it comes to movement, what's good for one may not feel great to someone else. Some people need to really sweat and work hard to feel like they're getting the most benefit. Others like to take it slower. If you decide to join a gym, there is certainly a class or a piece of equipment that's just right for you. Swim, pedal, walk, stretch, bounce, jump, play tennis, hit a ball, walk a dog, just MOVE! Do it inside or out but find something that feeds your soul and do it. I promise you'll be so glad you did.

Okay, I've talked about movement and its importance in our daily lives. Now let's look at the three main areas of movement, why each is important to our lasting health and how we can incorporate all of them. Let's begin with the obvious one, aerobic. We all get some form of aerobic movement just by moving our bodies everyday. But let's be honest, most of us could be getting more. Aerobics does so many wonderful things for us! It protects our heart by pumping more blood per beat, thus decreasing heart rate. It helps lower blood pressure and increases our good HDL cholesterol while reducing high blood triglycerides. It contributes to weight loss, which in turn leads to a reduction in many diseases. It improves our mood and helps us to sleep more soundly. And here's an eye opener for you! Are you too tired to move your body more? It turns out, the more movement you incorporate into your life, the more energy you will feel. It's true! Aerobics increases our body resistance, which in turn, increases our sense of well-being.

I always feel great after I do some form of work out but I've noticed over the years that the more tired I am before my work out, the better I feel when I'm done. I end up with tons of energy that I didn't have before. So, the times you least feel up to it, those are the perfect times to jump in and do it. Does this sound like a familiar scenario to you? You think, I am so exhausted I don't feel like doing anything. What if I told you that I know that feeling? I've been there. Wouldn't you love to get rid of this feeling? Taking it easy and sleeping more hasn't helped. What if I told you that you will feel different after you get your body moving? You've got nothing to lose and everything to gain. What do you say? Hopefully, now you say, I'm in! It's worth a shot! I'm worth a shot! Okay, now that you've decided to begin, let's talk about all the options available out there.

First of all, it's a wonderful time now for anyone trying to become more active. Even just a few short years ago, there were not a lot of options for gyms and those that were around were very much alike. We have outdoor structured work-outs now for those who want to be outside, we have work-outs on the water and we have functional training that prepares you for the movements you perform in everyday life. The options are plentiful and I encourage you to explore your opportunities. I have programs ranging from belly dancing to aerial arts school available to me right here in my own community. Let's list a few forms of aerobic movement that you can begin to take advantage of now. Walking, running, bicycling (road and mountain), spinning classes, boot camps, jump roping, step classes, stair climbing, elliptical trainers and swimming are all good choices. All of these activities use large muscle groups for a sustained amount of time. Try to perform one for 30 to 60 minutes three to five times a week and mix it up so that you don't find yourself getting into a rut. You can join a gym, you can sign up for local training events or you can simply step out and begin your walk or your hike. It's all up to you!

Strength training is the second form of necessary movement for our bodies. Why? Simply put, it reduces body fat by increasing lean muscle and bone mass, both of which decrease with age. You will help control your weight because muscle burns calories more efficiently than fat. Bone density will increase by stressing your bones, decreasing your risk of osteoporosis. You'll boost your stamina as you gain strength. All of these things will help us to age successfully, hopefully disease free. At the very least, these effects will prevent the frailty that we so often consider a normal part of the aging process.

Strength training probably conjures up images of bulky men and heavy weight equipment. It certainly can mean this but that's just one scenario. Resistance bands and kettle balls have become widely incorporated in most formal classes in the last few years and you can purchase your own to use at home if that's a better option for you. You can also buy a few select free weights or weights that you can attach pieces to so that they can become varying amounts of weight. Don't know where to begin? There are a ton of books and DVD's available for purchase. One that you may find helpful is Shred It With Weights by Jillian Michaels. You can get it in book or DVD form and included in it, are two thirty- minute workouts using a kettle ball or single hand weight. I particularly like the fact that she has modifications for true beginners. Still doesn't sound right for you? You simply use your own body weight to derive the benefits. Pushups, pullups, abdominal crunches, squats and lunges are all great options. If you're still struggling with where to begin or feel that you need an extra boost, you can always hire a trainer to plan out a good routine for you and then you'll be able to do it on your own. Some trainers even come to your home if you don't want to go to the gym.

Lastly, we need to maintain our balance and flexibility. This is especially important as we age in order to avoid those aches and creaks that we hear our parents or grandparents complain about. We also want to avoid falls and if they do occur we want to be able to bounce back from them. If you're comfortable with using equipment, exercise balls and balance balls are especially helpful. Again, you can call on the expertise of a personal trainer to guide you here or you can buy a video or even an instructional book to learn effective techniques for yourself.

Tai chi is an ancient practice that can help you to maintain and even increase flexibility. It also offers a wonderful form of relaxation and centeredness. There is a beautiful flow of movement within this practice and you may want to try it for yourself. Along these lines, both Pilates and yoga offer their own benefits. Let's begin with yoga. Another ancient practice, yoga can change your physical as well as your mental capacity. It can be a key player in maintaining long-term health and its use of meditation and breathing techniques can help you with your inner shift. During your practice, you let go of all the thoughts racing through your mind and all of the items on your to do list. You focus instead on the movement and on your breath. Developing a regular yoga practice has transformed life for many, many people. And keep in mind there are several styles of yoga to suit different needs. It's for every age and every level. There is hatha yoga, power yoga, relaxation yoga, prenatal yoga, and bhakti yoga to name a few. If you're just beginning your practice, hatha yoga is an ideal place to start. And within this branch, there are a number of styles. So if you try a class and it really doesn't seem to be a good fit, don't give up. Just try another style. You'll find the one that's right for you. If and when you are ready for a deeper practice, Bikram or "hot yoga" may be your next yoga style. This class consists of twenty-six postures, most of which are held for at least ten seconds. These classes also emphasis leg strength and balance by holding a series of one-legged standing postures in the first half of each class. It is worth noting here that depending on your chosen style, yoga can build your core strength and build muscle as well. Yoga's total benefits are far too numerous to discuss here but I just want you to be aware of it and open yourself up to its possibility for you.

One final form of movement worth mentioning is that of Pilates. This practice was developed by Joseph Pilates in the early 20th century and was practiced mainly by dancers in specialized studios. Today, it's found in community centers, gyms and Pilates studios. It focuses on core strength and this is obtained through concentration, control and centering. Your powerhouse is your abdomen, lower and upper back, hips, buttocks and inner thighs. All movement begins from this powerhouse and flows outward to the rest of your body. Pilates demands focus. The way the exercises are done is more important than the exercises themselves. And unlike other practices, the exercises don't get easier over time. Because as you focus harder you take your practice to deeper levels and this requires more effort. Breath plays a significant role as this practice attempts to coordinate the Pilates breath with each exercise. Many participants practice this on a mat with no special equipment. However, there are devices called reformers available at some facilities that can deepen your practice. You can expect greater strength without the bulk. Think long lean muscles. You will also experience increased flexibility, development of core strength, improved posture and increased energy. As with many forms of movement that we've talked about, Pilates can increase our awareness of mind-body connection.

I hope you're gaining a sense of the importance of movement in your life. It's about more than losing those added pounds or doing it because you think you should. Don't do it out of guilt or obligation. You probably won't enjoy it and you'll likely abandon it eventually. Do it because you truly want to. It's about your physical health; it's about your psyche. It's about your peace of mind; it's even about your happiness. Explore all of the possibilities and find the ones that resonate with you. I promise when you do, you'll look forward to it, you'll even come to depend on it and you'll wonder how you lived without it for so long.

Finding Your Passion and Purpose

"The day came when the risk
to remain tight in the bud was
more painful than the risk it
took to blossom."
—ANAIS NIN

CHAPTER THREE

Here You Are!

What's Holding Me Back?

Let's talk about what we all do to get the bills paid, shall we? Many of us have no idea what we want to do as we make our way through school. There are those lucky few who do and those who are unsure but fall into a profession that they love. But I think for most of us, we're somewhere in between. We have jobs that are okay. Our coworkers are nice and maybe we have an understanding boss. Of course, there are many others who dread their jobs and actually experience physical symptoms the night before they have to start a new workweek. Still others choose to stay home and take care of the family. Some in this situation love it and thrive. Others may find it challenging and experience it as a struggle. Whoever you are and whatever you do, I want you to be happy with your choice and it is a choice. Regardless of how long you've been in your chosen role or what got you there, this is your life and your time to share your unique gift.

It took me a long time to have the courage to leave my sales position. I was very successful at it and I enjoyed the daily interaction with many different people. But the products I was representing didn't align with my core values and so for a long time, I felt like a fraud. Doctor's offices and hospitals were my assigned "targets" and so I came into contact with many people who had health issues. I made it a point everyday to connect with as many people as I could to make their day a little brighter and to help them out whenever I could. But still, my actual reason for being there was not something I was enjoying, nor did I necessarily agree with it. So what was holding me back from leaving?

I think I always knew what it was that was preventing me from making that change. It's the same thing that keeps many of us trapped in professions that end up making us feel unfulfilled, bored, or downright miserable. And that thing is fear: fear of failure, fear of change, fear of being judged, fear of not having enough money. These are all valid fears but at the same time they are fears that we magnify and use as crutches to justify our inaction.

Say Hello to Your Fears

Let's look at the fear of failure first. What is it exactly that you think you're going to fail at and why? Are you not smart enough, young enough, tough enough, or flexible enough? Do you feel like you already missed your window of opportunity? Maybe all the new technology has you running scared. Whatever the reason, I want you to take a deep look inside again and come up with your list of reasons for your fear of failure. When that's done, look at each one closely. Now, concentrate on the ones you can do something about. Would some classes help you? Maybe you could speak to someone who's doing something that's aligned with your vision. Do you have a vision? Ask questions that will generate new ideas. Get more familiar with some possible scenarios and you'll get more comfortable. You know, sometimes when we really start to do some digging, things aren't as difficult as they once appeared to be. Just begin the process!

Now, how about those reasons that reside a little deeper, the ones that are there but unseen? Maybe we choose not to see them. I ask you now to be brave and to see them. Because until we recognize them and accept them, there is nothing we can do to eliminate them. When you do acknowledge them, they'll stop haunting you. You see them for what they are. Just as you have created them, you can be rid of them. Here's an idea. Why don't you write each of their names down on a piece of paper and then create your own ritual to destroy them. Not young enough? Poof, good-bye! We need to stop the critic inside all of our heads. It doesn't matter what size you are, how old you are or how smart you are. We all have a unique gift that is ours alone to share and we are all perfect in our imperfection. Know that you are an amazing human being and get out there and start sharing!

How about this fear of change? It's such a universal fear yet change is woven into the fabric of our lives. Nothing stays the same so why do we fight so hard against it? Is it fear of the unknown? What's the worst that can happen? Is your life so perfect now that anything new would pale in comparison? You and I both know that's probably not the case yet we cling to the familiar with every ounce of our being. It may not be the best, it may not make us happy but at least we are safe. Really? Is that what we want to be? Sure, it's wonderful to be safe but how about safe and fulfilled at the same time? That's the very least we should expect of our lives.

Maybe you have no energy left. You're not happy with your situation but you've resigned yourself to the fact that this is your life. This is the path you followed and now you're going to ride it out until you can retire. I promise you: That energy that has left you has left because you have given up on yourself. You need something to look forward to, to plan, to envision and then bring it to fruition. The energy is there. It's just waiting for something to do. Find your dream, your passion and the energy will follow. You will wake up and wonder why you waited so long to make your change.

Remember the feeling you had when you first fell in love? I don't know about you but I suddenly had all the energy in the world. I needed less sleep and everything about my world was clearer. Colors were more vivid, smells were stronger and I was just so… glad and grateful to be alive! Aside from the obvious hormonal reasons for this, what else is going on when we find that special someone? I believe we move outside of our own comfort zone and get rid of our protective layer. We get rid of our fears. We open ourselves up to someone else and they become part of our focus and inspiration. Their happiness is our happiness. When we discover our purpose and begin to act on it, we open ourselves up once again. We lose our fears and our vision becomes our focus and inspiration now. We stop focusing on all the things we can't do and instead, pour all of our renewed energy into this labor of love! It's no longer a matter of "if" we can do it or "should" we do it. It becomes instead "how" we'll do it because it is going to happen.

Are you afraid of what your friends and family will think if you leave your job? When I finally did it, lots of people thought I was crazy. People were getting laid off and here I was, actually giving up my job voluntarily. Some people, I suspect, even thought I was being selfish. But you know what? At the end of the day, it's your life and it's your choice. You and only you, have to live with this choice. It's up to each one of us to find our own happiness and discover what it is that will lead us to that happiness.

Every time I attempted to leave, I found a reason to stay. I even convinced myself for brief periods of time, that I could be happy doing this. But I always came back to that familiar gut feeling that I wasn't supposed to be here. As long as I stayed, I'd never find whatever it was that I was truly meant to do.

We all want people to like us and to respect us. I

totally get that. But consider this. When people tell you you're crazy or foolhardy for doing something, where do you think that opinion is coming from? Consider that these people are projecting their own fears onto you. Maybe they're not happy but they've never had the courage to do something different. Maybe they did attempt change at some point in their lives and failed. Could it be that some are a bit jealous of your bravery? I don't bring these things up to discredit anyone or question the reason behind their disapproval. It could very well be that the person telling you that you're crazy, does have your best interest at heart or at least they think they do. I bring it up because I want you to remember that we're all human and we all have our own personal issues that we deal with. Opinions can be narrow and skewed. So you need to block out all of the other voices coming at you and listen to your own voice. It's in there. You just have to be still long enough to hear it.

Lastly, let's look at the money fear. This is a valid fear. Let's be realistic: we all need enough money to pay our bills, save for our futures and have enough left over to enjoy our lives with vacations and things that bring us pleasure. I'm not suggesting that this shouldn't play a part in our decision making process. I am however, saying that we shouldn't let the fear itself keep us from making a change. Let's not just throw this out there as an easy excuse. Look at your finances. Do you have a budget? Will your spouse help support you if you do decide to do this? Have you figured out how much you need now versus what you want? What are some areas that you might be able to work with to lower your costs? Sometimes we have to take a small step back in order to take a giant step forward. Keep your vision in your head. Use it for motivation and allow it to propel you forward. Is your money situation looking good and you're still fearful? You've got it! You need to look in again!

Why do you still worry about the money even though you know it will in all likelihood be okay? Where is this fear coming from? Take the time to really think about this. It could be that it has nothing to do with your possible transition and everything to do with something that happened in your past. If you can identify this event and acknowledge it you'll likely be able to overcome the fear that it was creating in you: really devote time to this process. Lastly, if you do search and fail to come up with the source of your fear or if you just don't feel comfortable with the process, face it and move forward. Otherwise, you are letting this fear control you and hold you back.

Dictionary.com defines fear as a distressing emotion aroused by impending danger, evil, pain, etc. whether the threat is real or imagined. Fear can be a helpful emotion in that it readies us for action against this perceived threat. Even if our fears are imagined, they can make us even stronger by necessitating our mastery of them. What is the opposite of fear? Courage, security and calm all come to mind. And these are all obtained when we face our fear and move beyond it. When we have challenges such as fear to overcome in our journey, the rewards we receive when we finally arrive at our desired outcome are so much sweeter. And that is why we need our fears. We need to be pushed out of our apathy, out of our comfort zone in order to reach our true potential. No matter where you are at this moment or what you are doing, you are a part of the energy on our planet. You affect events and outcomes. We all do. So open up your heart and make that effect as beautiful and meaningful as you possibly can!

No matter where you are in your life right now, make it count for you; make it worthwhile. Find value and joy in whatever it is you're doing. Remember my sales position? Everyday I tried to touch the life of at least one person. One day I had a long discussion with an elderly woman who had brought her husband in to see the doctor for a breathing problem. But as I talked to her, she shared with me her fear of losing her husband to Alzheimer's. He had become increasingly more confused and argumentative and she wasn't sure what to do about it. As it happened, I knew of a wonderful resource for her and I gave her some contact information as well as some insights that I had gained from experiencing this very thing with a close family member myself. What if I hadn't known anything about Alzheimer's? What if I had no name to supply her with? It wouldn't have mattered. It wouldn't have changed the fact that someone had taken the time to listen to her, to hear her fears and make them real. I connected with her. I made a difference, no matter how small. I did many more things that day but this one thing made this day amazing and worthwhile.

We are presented with such opportunities every-day. Have you ever noticed someone who seems to be totally engaged and happy with what it is they're doing and wondered how that could be? I was riding one of those hotel buses at the airport once and the driver was extremely animated. He was laughing and greeting everyone who got on and he seemed oblivi-ous to all of the scowling faces not to mention the unbearable heat. I thought to myself, "This guy does this all day long, every day. And he probably doesn't make that much money. How can he be so happy?" I've come to realize that his happiness didn't come from his daily drives to and from the airport. In fact, I think he could have used this job as his excuse for be-ing unhappy and miserable. Instead of choosing to be miserable, he chose happiness. He chose happiness by interacting with all kinds of people every day, all day. He was connecting. He was sharing his optimism and making a difference. In so doing, he had connected with soul. How are you choosing to make your unique connection?

Finding Your Passion and Purpose

"Our greatest joy and our greatest pain comes in our relationships with others."
—STEPHEN COVEY

CHAPTER FOUR
Who Needs Friends?

There Goes My Calm!

Up until now we've been taking a look at ourselves and discovering ways that we can improve upon our lives in order to live our lives fully. Now we'll look at other people and how our interactions with those people affect us, or at least how we allow them to affect us. Let's face it, when we're alone it's so much easier to be the way we want to be, to feel that calm, centered sensation. We feel really good about ourselves, we feel content. We've got this, right?

I was feeling exactly that way one sunny Sunday morning. I was reading a book, sipping my tea and soaking in the warm sun streaming through my window on that spring day. My cat was sitting nearby, purring loudly in pure contentment. And then my phone rang. It was my friend Chris again. She had been divorced from her husband for several years now and he was a great father to her two boys. Yet whenever she spoke of him, you got the feeling that it just happened recently, as she held so much anger and resentment for such a long time. I had several conversations with her over the course of our two year friendship, with each talk trying to help her to move on. But it never worked. Here I was again, listening to her complain about him and complain about his new wife. Nothing he did was good enough and nothing in her life was worthy of being happy about. She didn't have many friends and frankly, it was because she was so negative that no one wanted to be around her. I thought that with my continued support and friendship, she would eventually get over her resentment and fill her life with more joy. Yet here I was again, listening to her and feeling my stomach knotting up! I could feel myself getting tense as my frustration grew. I knew nothing I said would change her perceptions. I was beginning to feel like she actually enjoyed being miserable and I was becoming resentful. This is not how I envisioned my day going at all! I listened but offered no advice or opinion and I kept the call reasonably short. Still, when it was over I could feel a shift. I started to think about her and then about other negative events in my life. Consequently, my resentment grew because I felt like she dumped all of her negativity on me so that she could feel better.

The Stuff of Life

This is just one example of something that happens to every one of us. We don't live in a bubble. We're subjected to jealous friends, nosy neighbors, demanding spouses, meddling relatives, and a host of other challenging associations. We are also subjected to our own internal associations such as our jealousy, our insecurity, and our negativity. We're trying our best but we're all human and as such we are constantly evolving. It is how we deal with these associations that define us.

Learning which relationships serve us and which ones don't is a hard lesson to learn. It can be challenging and painful but it is one that we must learn if we are to live this life fully and with as much joy as we can. There is a beautiful essay written by author Jean Dominique Martin that attempts to bring us a greater understanding of our various relationships and why some come to an end. Relationships are grouped into those that are formed for a reason, for a season and for a lifetime. It is the author's belief that when we figure out which one it is, we will know what to do for each person. It has helped me to make sense of some of my previous relationships and given me a broader perspective on all of them. I'd like to share my interpretation of this essay with you in hopes that you too, will gain clarity and understanding.

When people come into your life for a Reason, it's to fulfill a specific need or a desire that you've expressed. These are the people who are in your life for the shortest period of time and they are there for the express purpose of assisting and guiding you to reach your desire or to overcome an obstacle. They may assist you physically, spiritually or emotionally. And then one day, through no fault of your own, the relationship ends. Perhaps the person walked away, perhaps they died or maybe they acted in such a way that you decided to end the relationship. Know that in these instances, all is well. Your need has been met. The purpose of the relationship has been fulfilled so you can look back on it with fond memories. People who come into your life for a Season are now giving you the opportunity to learn and to grow. They may teach you a new skill or a different way of thinking. Perhaps they share their insights with you and open up a whole new world of opportunity for you. They may bring you joy and happiness or they may be the very ones who cause you pain and despair. But each of them is there to enable you to expand your being. They too, will eventually disappear from your life. They are meant to be with you only until your learning with them is complete. Lastly, there are those who are with us throughout our lives, our Lifetime relationships. These are the people who have the greatest impact on our development. We learn coping strategies and build our emotional strength through these relationships. We love these people and accept them for who they are. It's not always smooth, but we hang in there and we continually work on it. We question, we soul search, we grow.

I hope this brings you some clarity in regards to your relationships, both past and present. For you see, if you understand that every person that comes into your life, comes into it for a reason, you'll learn to accept them and understand their meaning, even those people that seem to have created so much pain and chaos. Without that pain, you wouldn't have learned something that you needed to learn. You wouldn't have grown to the degree that you needed to in order to fulfill your destiny. Each person you meet is a gift and it's the very ones who seem to cause you the most pain who are your greatest gifts.

Relationships are unique and complicated and

multi-layered. It would be impossible for me to offer my interpretations or advice on any given one without knowing the specific circumstances nor would it be helpful to you. We need to learn for ourselves the intricacies of each relationship and how best to navigate them. There are some valuable lessons that I have learned along the way however, that I feel are universal ones. They are lessons that I've learned through my own sometimes, painful journey and it is my hope that they will help you as you journey through yours.

The first of these lessons is that of personal boundaries. These can be defined as guidelines, rules or limits that a person creates to identify for themselves what are reasonable, safe and permissible ways for other people to behave around him or her and how they will respond when someone steps outside those limits. Simply stated, we are responsible for our happiness and we need to be proactive every day in order to maintain it. Let's go back to my friend Chris and her untimely phone call. I was in a negative space after that call. I allowed my conversation with her to change my peaceful mood. What could I have done differently? For starters, I could have stopped being so readily receptive to her complaints and grievances. We all have our lows and we've all counted on a close friend to listen to us as we recount our experiences of betrayal or wrong- doing. It helps to verbalize things sometimes and as we verbalize, we hopefully begin to heal. But when someone repeatedly whines and complains, they're not ready or willing to heal. Their complaints have become their reality, their accepted way of existing. We're not going to help them or change them by allowing or nurturing this behavior. In my case, a long overdue discussion eventually ensued. I told her that that she had a wonderful home with two beautiful sons. She was in a profession that she loved. She was healthy and had no financial burdens. I wanted to be her friend but I wouldn't listen to her complaints any longer. It was that simple. If she started rehashing old wounds, I could not be present for it. Whether she sought counseling for this, found someone else to complain to or just wallowed in it, was not for me to decide.

We are only responsible for our own actions and behavior. Set your boundaries lovingly but clearly and stick to them. How can you expect your friends and family to respect your boundaries if you haven't set any for them?

I have adopted another practice that I find invaluable in maintaining my sense of self. And it's really quite simple. That is, I don't discuss something that's bothering me about a friend or family member with anyone but that person. It can be hard to have an honest conversation with someone about something that they did or didn't do that resulted in your unhappiness. But if this conversation comes from a place of truth, integrity and love, it will serve the relationship. It will keep it honest and hopefully, will strengthen it. Similarly, I don't listen to someone else's complaints about someone else or if I do, I don't chime in and agree with them. I would also caution you about giving any advice, no matter how pure your intentions. This advice can be manipulated and misrepresented, resulting in hurt feelings and even more people with grievances! Encourage the person to have an honest conversation with the source of their unhappiness. Tell them that you're not comfortable speaking about the other person when they're not present to contribute to the conversation. You have set your boundaries and in doing so have most likely avoided more hurt and misunderstanding.

I strive everyday to stick to these boundaries and do I always succeed? Absolutely not! I have insecurities that can get triggered, old patterns that kick in and then there's always my darned ego that gets in the way. But the fact is I do try and more importantly I recognize it and acknowledge it when I fail. I simply try again. I do my best to always come from a place of love.

One of the reasons I can so easily accept my failures brings me to my second lesson, the lesson of acceptance. None of us is perfect and we needn't be. It's our very imperfections that make each of us unique. Embrace imperfection, both in yourself and in others. For yourself, learn to love the whole of you; the you who is strong and beautiful, the you who is fearful and unsure, the you who sometimes disappoints you and the countless other parts of you that exist. Because without all of these parts, you wouldn't be the person you are, a person worthy of love and happiness. Each and every one of us is worthy of these things, even the people that seem to annoy us and challenge us.

Try to see the good in everyone. It's really there, even in the most hurtful and bullying individuals. We don't know what's driving a person's behavior. What pain might they be enduring that's causing them to be so unkind? You know, sometimes I'll be out in a store or at an event and I'll see someone who looks absolutely miserable. They'll sometimes be scowling, other times they look totally disinterested in anyone around them. These are the very people who I try to make a connection to. I attempt to make eye contact and then say hello with a big smile. Sometimes I might make a comment about how challenging the crowds are or how cold or windy it is. It doesn't matter so much what I say. Rather it's that I'm trying to find a common thread with this stranger to make a connection. I try to be warm and on a really good day, I'll make someone laugh. Sometimes these people aren't miserable at all, they're just lonely. Each time we connect with someone in a loving way, we are helping them to shine the light of their life energy more brightly and in so doing, we are strengthening our own. I have a challenge for you. For one day, try to make eye contact with every person you see and say hello. Keep track of how many smiles you get. I promise you'll be pleasantly surprised. And even if that's not the case for you; if you made just one person smile or feel a connection, you have had an amazing day! You have made a difference.

Sometimes the very people we love and choose to spend much of our time with can be the most challenging in terms of acceptance. They test us, they frustrate us, and they can make us question our personal decisions and choices. But as we've learned, they're all there for a specific purpose and that purpose is to help us to grow. And we are there to do the same for them. Let's talk about those people who are in our lives not because we chose to include them but because we were born into a relationship with them. These are people we love but don't always like. They are our early years, our teachers, and our entire universe for a brief period of time. They will be a part of who we are no matter how much or how little we interact with them. They matter to us, even if we don't always acknowledge it. When we learn to accept each one of them for exactly who they are we will be the better for it.

Sometimes, we create certain expectations of our

loved ones. In the case of our parents, we expect them to always be there for us, perhaps to help us make the right choices or to help us pick up the pieces when our life seems to be crumbling around us. But for many of us, those expectations don't always get met. Some parents may be too busy or self-absorbed to help or even to see what it is you need from them. Others through bitter divorce may choose to abandon you altogether. Still others may genuinely care but for one reason or another, they too fall short. Parents are human. They are fallible and they are learning just as we all are. See them as they are and accept them. Please don't take on the burden of guilt if they have fallen short. It's not something you did or didn't do. It's not who you are or who you are not. People act out of their own reality, their own perceptions. And only they decide what that reality is.

The same holds true for your brothers and sisters, your sons and daughters. Do you have hopes that your talented son will one day play professional sports? Do you secretly pray that your daughter becomes a doctor? Perhaps you just want your child to be happy, to find that special person and have an amazing family of their own. Maybe your talented son will suddenly lose interest in his chosen sport or your daughter will decide to forego college to pursue an acting career. It could happen that your child does find that special person and starts that amazing family only to find him or herself facing a divorce. Do you love them any less? Do you judge them? Do you blame yourself for the outcome? The answer in all cases is a resounding "no." Again, we are not responsible for the choices others make. We can try to help them, we can support them, make suggestions and lead by example but we cannot control the outcome. And no matter what path our loved ones choose, we see them for who they are not who we want them to be. We love them. We accept them.

We do choose our spouses, our life partners and this choice has one of the most profound effects on the trajectory our lives take. Being with a loving and supportive partner will certainly help us in becoming the best version of ourselves. Conversely, being with a critical and demanding partner can weaken us and take us on a detour from our chosen path. But this discussion is about acceptance so let's talk about those partners whom we've chosen to live with, those that may not meet our every need, our every expectation. These partners love us and we in turn, love them. We are happy for the most part but some days we just can't seem to connect with them. Maybe they seem distant; maybe they're so wrapped up in their job you feel like you're invisible to them. Some of you may be married to someone who never seems satisfied. Others of you could be with someone who is clingy and seems to drain your energy. Whatever the shortcoming, whatever the complaint or disappointment it is that you experience, if you have chosen to spend the rest of your life with this person it's because you saw something in this person. You felt it. You connected with it. Remember it. Look at all of the things you love about this person.

Acknowledge and accept. Take responsibility for your part in the relationship. If you want to feel needed, let them know they are needed. If you want to feel loved, love. They accept you as you are and you accept them. There will be good times and bad times. There will be events that will test your resolve and he or she will do something that angers you or has you questioning the relationship. I'll leave this lesson of acceptance with one final message. Remember this. People's actions have everything to do with them and nothing to do with you. When you see this, you will discover a new sense of peace within yourself.

Even with the best of intentions people hurt us. Sometimes they know they've hurt you and sometimes they have no idea of the pain that you may feel. It can be tough to forgive someone and it's especially hard to forgive if the offending person doesn't even acknowledge it. But forgive we must and that is my next lesson. When we forgive someone for something, we are letting go of the resentment and the anger. The forgiveness is in reality a gift to ourselves because we all want to feel good about life, after all. I've been hurt many times by people I love and I sometimes think to myself, "Why would this person do that to me? Don't they realize how hurtful it is or do they just not care?" I don't always get my answer but I most often choose to believe that they don't know that they have offended me or at least they don't realize the extent of my hurt. Sometimes we give others too much credit for being aware. Many people are so wrapped up in their own lives, so busy worrying about themselves and so pre-occupied with everyday survival that they really don't have any idea of what they've done. I'm not saying the hurt you feel is not real. I am saying that if you choose to take this stance, you will feel abundantly more at peace with yourself and with the world in general.

There are different ways to forgive depending on each circumstance. Perhaps you choose to have an open discussion about your hurt; the person apologizes, you accept and move on. Maybe the other person reacts by telling you they meant nothing by it and that you're being too emotional or too sensitive. This one can really sting. But again, this is their reality. In all likelihood you're not going to change it. What you can change is your reaction to it. Accept it and then do whatever you need to do to get past it. Write a letter and really let them have it! Get it all out! Then, ceremoniously destroy it. Feel better? We don't necessarily forget these injuries to our psyche but we learn to accept them as part of life, to not feel their sting so much. Sometimes we know the other person probably has no idea that they've hurt us and we have two choices. We can make them aware of the hurt or just let it go. Whatever you need to do to feel okay with it is exactly what you should do. We don't always choose to remain in the presence of someone who has hurt us but we can still forgive them. If you do decide to end the relationship, say goodbye and send them love!

As difficult as it can be to forgive others, it is so much harder to forgive ourselves. We agonize over things we did in our past that we would never do now. We go over it in our minds and wonder what might have been if we had chosen to do something differently or chose not to do it at all. The reason it's so hard to accept our mistakes and forgive ourselves is because we are continually growing and who we are today is not who we were five, ten, or twenty years ago. So the you who stands here today would never make such a careless error but guess what? The you who was around then really didn't know any better. You need to actively envision different versions of yourself over the course of your life. This enables you to step outside of yourself, to let your ego get out of the way so that you can understand and forgive. When you know better, you do better. Holding on to regret and self blame is a sure fire way to stall your life. You may even believe on some level that you don't deserve to be happy. We all deserve to be happy and whole. This is our purpose, our birthright. So, ease up on yourself. Everyday is a new day with limitless possibilities!

Relationships are fluid. They can be wonderfully satisfying one minute and challenging the next. They're good and bad, they're up and down; they're simple and complex. They are the stuff of life. We need relationships in order to develop and grow fully into the person we are meant to be. Even with all the challenges they certainly present us with, they are there for our benefit, and for our growth. The relationship that we have inside of ourselves is the most important one of all. Without a successful relationship with self, we have no chance of healthy relationships with others. So smile, lighten up! It's not that bad and even if it is, it's going to get better. Laugh! Laugh at yourself, at your silly mistake or your comical look. Laugh at your crazy kitten or your goofy dog. I have very few days without laughter. It's good for your psyche; it's good for your health; and it's contagious!

Don't you think everybody could use a little more

laughter in their lives? Laughter comes from the ability to let go, to drop the facade, the protective layer that so many of us wear. Why do we try so hard to project a different version of ourselves? Are you fearful that if you do expose your authentic self that you will be rejected? If that happens, then what are you supposed to do? Perhaps early on, this exact scenario played itself out and you've been hiding out securely ever since. Can I let you in on a secret? When you learn to accept yourself, even with all of your perceived flaws, your insecurities will disappear. Keep in mind that many, many people are walking around doing the exact thing you're doing. They're hiding! They too, may very well be insecure and unsure. Listen, everyone is not necessarily going to like you or want to be friends with you. But if you are open and true to yourself, people will see that and they will respect it. Not only that but when you're open and genuine, others can sense this and it gives them permission to do the same. So you see, by being brave enough to just relax and be yourself, you're allowing others that same freedom. You are sharing your gift! You are a catalyst for planting the seeds of understanding.

Finding Your Passion and Purpose

"Spirituality is your original face;
it is the discovery of your
intrinsic nature."
—OSHO

CHAPTER FIVE

In a Church or in a Forest

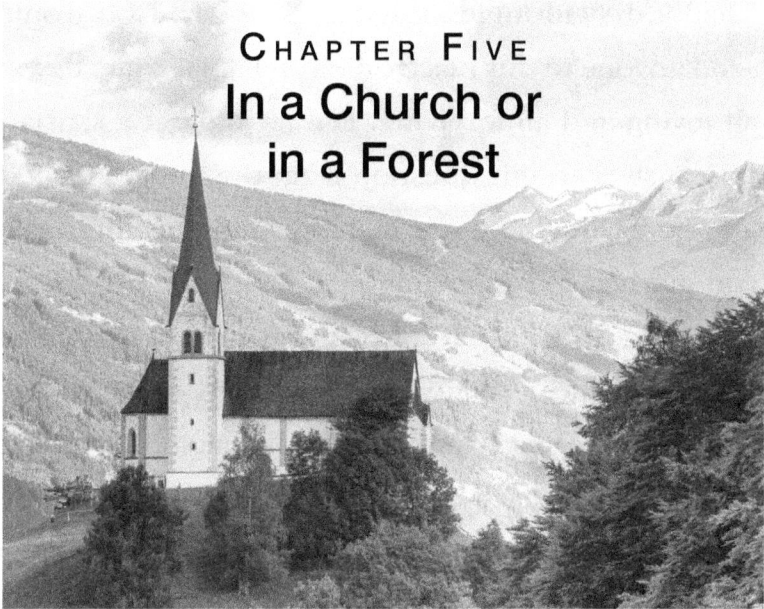

Is There Really a Hell?

I grew up in a large Catholic family with lots of love and laughter. I attended Catholic school until I entered a public high school at which point I was suddenly exposed to a whole new world, one that made me question some of the beliefs that had been instilled in me throughout my early education. I've always had an inquisitive mind and from an early age

I had a difficult time understanding why God would send anyone to this place called Hell if He indeed, was all loving and all forgiving. I never did get a satisfactory answer to this question from the nuns. In fact, I got the feeling that I was making them uncomfortable and maybe even annoying them a bit.

I did stay with Catholicism until my early thirties at which time I abandoned organized religion altogether. I have since studied various religions and have found merit in each one. However, no single religion has totally resonated with me. So I suppose I belong to that percentage of the population who experience spirituality on a more personal level. One major epiphany I experienced along the way is that for me, God is within all of us. And by God I mean whatever it is you believe God to be. Even for you atheists among us, don't you feel there is a connection between all of us; an energy if you will? I find great strength and comfort in this notion of connectedness, that none of us is truly ever alone. My purpose in discussing this is not to persuade you one way or another in regards to your own beliefs in this area. It's merely to give you a glimpse into mine.

What Is Spirit?

I feel strongly in my core that we all need to believe in something outside of ourselves. It takes us from a "me" centered mentality to a "we" centered mentality. Yes, it's important to focus on yourself and to nurture your growth. But why is it so important? It's important because if each one of us is not strong enough, centered enough, or loved enough, then how can we possibly share our gift with the rest of the world? And isn't that what we're all here to do, each in our unique way? Some will make great waves (think Oprah) while others may create the tiniest of ripples but together we create the entire sea. The sum of all of our parts creates the whole, creates change, movement, progress, growth. Begin to think in terms of family when you think of every human being. It will bring you comfort and a sense of belonging.

I ask you now the question I asked you at the very beginning of this book but now in terms of spirituality. What do you believe? It doesn't matter what your answer to this question is. What does matter is that you have taken the time to carefully consider this question and that you know in your soul that it's true for you. This belief will guide you and steady you when you're challenged. You will be more sure footed along your path.

What exactly is spirituality? According to Diction-ary.org, spirituality is the state or quality of being dedicated to god, religion, or spiritual things or values, esp. as contrasted with material or temporal ones. Religion is an important part of existence for millions of people. It can offer strength to grow, guidance when you're unsure, comfort from grief and a safe haven when you're feeling lost or alone. If you are one of the millions of people who are part of a religious institution, you have found what is true for you. You have defined your beliefs.

Still, we are all spiritual beings and whether we are part of an organized religion or not, our spirituality defines us and guides us. Where do you find spirit? Where do you feel it, sense it? Maybe you believe this isn't true for you, that you've never had such an experience. When I am in spirit, I feel a sense of calm, of completeness, of surrender. I am immersed in the moment and every cell in my being is connected and alive. I have no doubt, no nagging questions; I have no confusion. Sometimes, I seek out these experiences through such methods as yoga or meditation. Other times, spirit just decides to offer me the gift of its presence. These moments are wonderful and unexpected. But I believe they happen because in those moments my mind is uncluttered and focused.

Much like everything else we've been discussing, in order to feel spirit, we need to be aware and to be still. Spirit is always with us but it's only when we slow down and take the time to look and to listen, that we are aware of its presence. Do you still feel like you haven't had this experience? Have you ever held a newborn? Does anything else exist outside of that face, those tiny fingers, at that moment? Have you walked a beach and gazed out at the ocean, looked at its beauty and completeness? Have you ever been so involved in something that you're doing or creating, that time seems to have stopped for you? Have you looked at your dog whose staring at you with pure love and devotion and felt that bond? Have you ever been with someone who is dying? When you were a child, did you lie in the snow and create snow angels? Have you ever looked up at the sky and created images for each cloud?

Grace is present in all of these instances. There are so many more and they're always there for us. What is the common thread within all of these things? Each of them is enough for us in the moment. Each is complete and receives our full awareness. Each is the only thing that exists for us in that moment. Our lives are richer when we pause to allow grace to enter. Try to be more aware as you go about your day. You can find grace in the eyes of a man peddling for spare change on a street corner. Be ready; be open!

For me, spirituality is synonymous with nature. Who can walk through a forest of redwoods without feeling a sense of awe and inspiration? Is it possible to look at one single flower and not feel something outside of yourself? Flowers in nature enable plants to reproduce by producing their seeds. All of nature is in perfect order, each one with a distinct purpose for existence. This is creation right before our eyes and has continued throughout time, completing its cycles again and again. Even through the longest, snowiest winters, we know that when spring arrives, the cro-cuses will be pushing their way out towards the light. Nature is life itself and we need to experience it to fully experience our own. Have you ever walked along a beach and felt the difference when you decided to take off your sandals and walk barefoot through the sand? There's something about the feel of the sand under my feet that I find very grounding and I have never been able to resist it, even on a cold day at the end of winter.

Many of us have become disconnected from this feeling. We live in an artificial world, especially now in this 21st century. We talk to each other through electronic devices, we spend more time than ever sit-ting in front of various screens and we somehow have managed to insulate ourselves from nature and from each other much of the time. It's no coincidence that we refer to nature as Mother Nature. Just as a mother nurtures her child, the earth nurtures us by giving us what we need to live. In the American Indian culture, there exists an Earth Mother that provides the water of life that gives them the provision of food. If you look up the definition of nature, you will find that the word is derived from the Latin word, natura or essential qualities. And in the Latin Dictionary, natura is defined as birth, character, nature. To reconnect with yourself, reconnect to nature.

Have you been fortunate enough to share your life with an animal? I have and I give much of the credit for my growth to these beautiful souls. They teach me to live in the moment; they love me unconditionally and they demonstrate a purity that I believe exists in all animals. For 16 years I shared mine with a cat named Christopher. Though there is a place in my heart for all the animals that have touched my life, Christopher was the one who I connected with on a deep soul level. It's hard to put into words the intensity of the bond or the extent of our mutual understanding and those of you who have not shared your life with such an animal may even find the notion of this absurd. But for those of you who are fortunate enough to have such an animal in your life, you know exactly what this amazing gift is. It opens your heart, it creates a shift in your consciousness, and it forever changes you for the better.

You see, spirit is all around us. It is in the air we

breathe. It is in our moments of silence. It is the gentle whisper of the wind in your hair. It's not an ethereal deity so far removed that you just can't seem to grasp its existence. It is you and it is me. We are spiritual beings living in this material world. Stay awake and aware and you will know what it is you believe in terms of your own spirituality.

"Your visions will become clear
only when you can look into
your own heart. Who looks
outside, dreams; who
looks inside, awakes."
—C.G. Jung

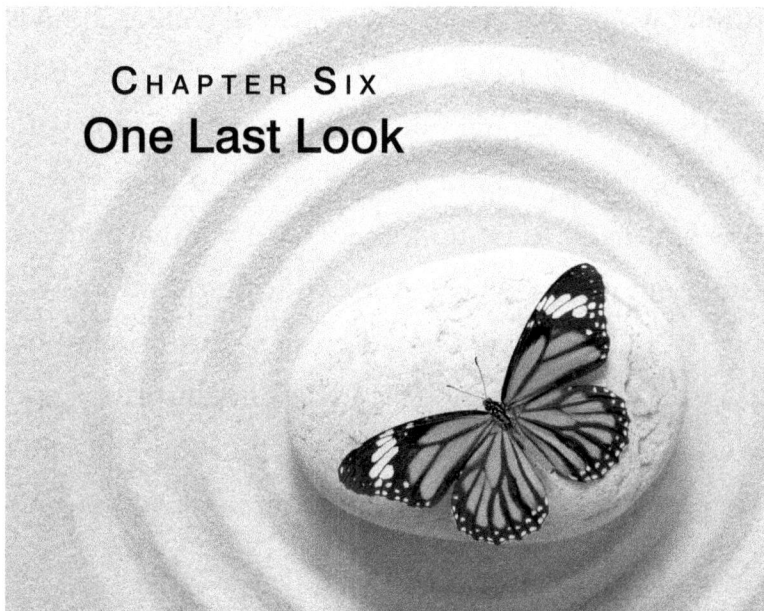

CHAPTER SIX
One Last Look

Where Are You Now?

What are you feeling right now? Happiness? Frustration? Skepticism? No matter what it is you're feeling, I hope that a process has begun for you, no matter how small, of beginning to look a little deeper, of noticing a shift in your perspective, and of experiencing a new sense of curiosity about the world around you and your place in it. It doesn't matter what you're doing. What does matter is how you're feeling about it. Remember the airport bus driver? His enthusiasm for life can truly become one in which you identify with. Only you know where it is you need to be and what it is you need to be doing. Some of you have merely forgotten it somewhere along your journey. Have you been looking as you've made your way through these pages? Let's revisit these areas of life and see where you are. Really think about each question and allow yourself the time to answer thoughtfully and honestly.

Food: Are you feeling good about your food choices right now? Do you feel like you have the necessary information to make the right choices for yourself or at least a guideline to build upon? If you feel you're eating too much of the wrong foods have you asked yourself what it is you're really hungry for? Is it the food or is it something more? Are you eating your food mindfully and taking pleasure in its preparation? Enjoy your meals! Try new foods! Remember, food is one of life's wonderful pleasures. It is fuel; it is nourishment. It is life itself. Please don't allow it to be a source of stress or confusion for you. If you feel like you want to learn more about it, go for it! There's a lot of information available to you and if you read enough and gain enough knowledge you'll be able to form your own conclusions and know what's right for you.

Movement: How often are you moving your body? How much time are you sitting? If you sit at a desk for your job, are you moving on your breaks? Have you taken the time to really think about how you want to incorporate movement into your life? If you have, have you taken any steps to begin the process? Do you find yourself resisting? If you do, ask yourself "why."

What's going on for you? Are you afraid you won't be good at something? Maybe deep down you think you don't deserve it or maybe you're holding on to something that needs to be released. Tough stuff, I know! But you owe it to yourself to go there, to look inward, so that you can enjoy the wonderful feeling of living in a fit body.

Find your niche. It may change over time but I promise, once you incorporate movement into your life on a regular basis, you'll wonder how you ever lived without it. It will carry you into your elder years without much of the discomfort and disease experienced by many.

Career/Life Choice: What are you doing right now? Are you enjoying it? Do you feel like you're making a difference? Are you a corporate executive? Maybe you're a sales associate. Perhaps you're a stay at home mom. Again, it doesn't matter what it is you're doing. Ask yourself, "Am I happy right now? Do I feel comfortable? Do I look forward to each day?" If you do, great! If not, have you taken the time to figure out why? Is there something about whatever it is you're doing that could be tweaked in some way to make it something worthwhile for you? If your answer is no, how have you begun the process of transition? What steps have you taken to make it happen? Do you have any idea what it is you want to do? If you're unhappy and yet you've done nothing, why is that? What's blocking you? What are you afraid of? What will happen if you do make your move? Look at your unique situation and take the time to begin to figure it all out. There are several agencies, probably right in your own community, that can help guide you. Seek them out. Do your research. Most people reinvent themselves at some point in their lives. It can be an exciting time and one of tremendous growth. Take the time to make it happen for you!

Relationships: Here's a challenging one for most of us. Have you taken the time to think about this? Do you know which relationships are nurturing you and which ones are draining you? Have you identified any areas of concern and if you have, what steps have you taken to improve them? Have you taken a real look at yourself and how you contribute to each of your relationships? If you're holding on to a relationship and you feel it's unhealthy, have you asked yourself why you stay? Again, what are your fears? Are you acting out of this fear and not out of love? Have you managed to get your ego out of the way when you're hurt or angry? We are social beings. We thrive on interacting with each other; we need each other. Our relationships are not static. They change and evolve and we need to tend to each one as they do. Have you taken some time to be alone with your thoughts? Our relationship with self is the key to developing and maintaining satisfying unions with others. Be conscious of all of these things. Don't take your relationships for granted and above all, enjoy them!

Spirituality: Have you always known what it is you believe to be true in regards to spirituality? Do you even know what spirituality is? Has your belief faltered or shifted over time? Have you no opinion and at this point don't know what you believe? As I've said before, it doesn't matter what it is you believe but that you believe in something. Believing in something outside of ourselves helps us to grow and belong to something much greater than ourselves. It allows us to feel a connection, a sense of belonging. If this area of your life is clear for you, I hope it continues to nourish you. If you feel you need religion in your life and you're not a member of any particular faith now, perhaps you can start to look into your choices and see what faith resonates with you. If organized religion is not what you seek and you're still unsure about your spirituality, take the time to be still and give this your focus and attention. It is a part of who you are and it is worth visiting.

All of these areas of your life have an impact on it and now that you've looked at all of them, REALLY looked at them, what can you expect to happen? How will this help move your life forward in a positive way?

Hopefully, you've been practicing being thoughtful and still, you may have uncovered some hidden fears and you've started to take steps, however small, to gain health, clarity and balance in your life. There is another factor that plays a part in our development that is worth mentioning here and that factor is time. Time affects each of us based on our own perception of it. Why is it that depending on what it is we're doing, thirty minutes can sometimes feel like an hour and at other times it seems to pass with lightening speed? After all, thirty minutes is thirty minutes, right? Here's where it gets interesting. Turns out, we may perceive time based on what kinds of information our brains are receiving. Some neuroscientists now believe that when we receive large amounts of information, it takes our brains a while to process all of it. The longer this processing takes the longer that period of time feels. That could explain why the older we get, the faster time seems to pass. We have processed so much information that much of it isn't new to us. So, this information is processed much more quickly and we are left with the feeling that life for us is passing by quickly as well.

This is all very interesting stuff but what's it got to do with our growth? Well, I believe that the concept of time (especially lack of it) can become a barrier for many of us. I also believe it can be determined by our unique experience or perception of it. We give it far too much control over our lives. You want to do something but it's not the right time. Why is this? When is the right time? Sometimes the right time never seems to come. Could it be that we are actually creating this conundrum by placing barriers in the way of our own happiness and success? One of the biggest reasons we have for not taking that leap is that we think it's too late. And that reason is not reserved for those who are far beyond their youth. It's a misguided belief uttered by many of us no matter what our age. Why do we place limitations on ourselves? No matter how old or young you are, no matter what you're doing or where you are, now is the perfect time to begin. None of us is guaranteed a future beyond this moment so in the words of Mahatma Gandhi, "Live as if you were to die tomorrow. Learn as if you were to live forever."

You might be thinking: Why should I start a new career or get a college degree? Why should I make any change at all? Now I'm talking to those of you who really believe that you're too old and that for the time and effort that you're going to have to put into this, you won't reap the benefits long enough. I have two thoughts for you. The first is that again, no one is guaranteed anything beyond this moment. You could be twenty years old and not be here tomorrow. Please get this limiting notion of time out of your mind. Secondly, you could pursue your dream and hope for the best. You could learn something new each day and look forward to the next. What if for some unforeseen reason your worst fear was realized and your life ended abruptly? Did you waste your time? Did you make a mistake? I think you know the answer to that. You lived every day to the fullest. You were happy and engaged in life. It doesn't matter whether you lived for another twenty years or another twenty months. Do you see? It's all about living today, REALLY living each and every day. Abraham Lincoln once said: "And in the end, it's not the years in your life that count. It's the life in your years." It's not the destination but the journey to reach it that really matters. So if you're letting this be a roadblock for you, let it go! It means nothing. It's a self-imposed illusion. Take your first step. Others will follow.

Finally Home

I spent so much of my life searching and questioning and after all of it, I finally feel a sense of certainty, a sense that I'm exactly where I'm supposed to be. How did I reach this point in my life? It wasn't any one particular choice that I made but rather a thoughtful process of finding my balance. I believe that in order to be fulfilled, we need to be aware of our gift so that we can share it. That's why we're here, after all. And in order to identify this gift we need to be in balance. When I look back over my life, there was always something out of balance. At one point, I was in an unhealthy relationship that continued for far too long. As I turned inward and really started to look into my life, I began to make changes; small shifts in consciousness that would forever change my direction. I have attempted to share some of my insights with you, in hopes that you too, will discover your gift.

The final piece came together for me when I finally left my sales position. How would I ever be able to reach my destination if I continued to do something that felt so far from who I really was? I was pouring all of my energy into this. There was nothing left. I needed to free up that energy to clear my mind and see my vision clearly. All of the things I've talked about here make you who you are. They are all necessary for you to be whole. When we are in balance, our energy is clear and that energy follows a path that leads you to your gift.

Have an open heart and an open mind. Be brave. Be fearless. Share. Explore. Question. Listen. Be willing to dig deep to find your answers. Look and take your leap! I wish you much love and light on your journey.

Look Deep and Leap

Bibliography

Eagleman, David M., and Alex O. Holcombe. *"Causality and the Perception of Time."* Trends in Cognitive Sciences 6.8 (2002): 323-25.

Massey, Paul. *The Anatomy of Pilates*. Nutbourne: Lotus Pub. 2009

Sarley, Dinabandhu, and Ila Sarley. *The Essentials of Yoga*. New York: Dell Pub. 1999.

Weil, Andrew. *Healthy Aging: A Lifelong Guide to Your Physical and Spiritual Wellbeing*. New York: Alfred A. Knopf, 2005.

Look Deep and Leap

About the Author

LORENA FIORE has been in Healthcare throughout her career, as a hospital nurse, a consultant, a lecturer, an educator and most recently an integrative health and wellness coach.

Her goal has always been to empower people to manage their health and to make informed decisions through education. Her special interest is in Integrative Medicine, encompassing mind, body and spirit.

Lorena offers her clients an opportunity to partner with her through a series of scheduled meetings. Together, they set goals and develop strategies that lead to life-long change for balance and health. For more information on Lorena's practice, visit: www.RealWithLorena.com.

Notes

Notes

Notes

Notes

Notes